Divine Dogs Online

Basenjis

Mychelle Klose

All Rights Reserved

Copyright © 2013 Mychelle Klose

All Rights Reserved .This book may not be reproduced, transmitted, or stored in whole or in part by any means, including graphic, electronic, or mechanical without the express written consent of the publisher except in the case of brief quotations embodied in critical articles and reviews.

This is the 49th book in Mychelle Klose's Pure Bred Dog Series

Published by Mychelle Klose

Copyright 2013 Mychelle Klose

http://www.divinedogsonline.com

http://www.facebook.com/divine.dogs.online

http://www.pinterest.com/divinedogsonlin

http://www.adoreyourdogbyvideo.com

http://www.dogtrainingbyvideo.com

Six months after your dog passes you still can't bear to talk about her. Yet, some may say, she was just a dog.

You reach under your bed and stumble across an old toy of hers and burst into tears. Yet she was just a dog.

After a long and mentally draining day at work, you'd give anything to be able to come home and just cuddle with her. Yet, she was just a dog.

Those who have never owned one, will never get it. That dog, was your friend, cuddle buddy, jogging partner, playmate, anxiety reliever, alarm clock, guard dog... etc

Just a dog, right?

by Emily Perez

- [Appearance](#)
- [Temperament](#)
- [Health](#)
- [How To Have A Healthy Dog](#)
- [Care](#)
- [Breeders](#)
- [Training](#)
- [Training Your Dog](#)
- [Origins](#)
- [Registries](#)

Be A Responsible Dog Owner

Dogs are very devoted, loyal and great friends with their owners. When you come home you can see the delight from your dog. He is so happy to see you. He loves to do anything you want to do even if it is just vegging on the couch. Owning a dog is a big commitment. You are responsible for this little bundle of fur for a long time. You have to feed him, train him, take him to the vet and make sure he stays healthy, keep him off the streets, keep him from disturbing the neighbors and many more responsibilities. Dog ownership is a long term financial and emotional commitment for up to 18 years with some breeds.

Is your lifestyle able to include a dog? Are you home enough to look after a dog? All dogs are different and you have to make sure that you get a dog that will fit into your lifestyle. If you are a runner you probably won't want a couch potato dog. If you don't like to vacuum don't get a dog that sheds a lot.

Decide what characteristics that you want in a dog. You have to decide on what size of dog you want, his temperament, guard dog or lap dog, energy level, how easy is he to train and how much grooming he will need. If you have picked the wrong dog and it doesn't fit into your lifestyle or family he could end up in an animal shelter looking for a new home. I am sure this is not what you want. Choose your dog carefully.

Spay and neuter your pets

Basenji

Dog Group: Hound

Height: Male 17 inches (43 cm) at the shoulder

Females 16 inches (40.6 cm)

Weight: Males 24 lbs (11 kg)

Females 22 lbs

Life Span: 10 to 12 years

Coat Colors: red, black, tricolor (black with tan in the traditional pattern) and brindle (black stripes on a background of red), all with white feet, chest and tip of tail

Appearance

The Basenji is a small dog. It looks very elegant and graceful. The body is square shaped, which means that they are as long as they are tall. They are very muscular and have a slender build. Their faces always seem to squint as if they are thinking deeply about something. The forehead is wrinkled. The ears are small, erect and pointed. The eyes are brown and almond shaped. The muzzle is short in length. The legs are long. The tail is tightly curled and is held up and over one side of the back. The coat is smooth, shiny, dense and short. It lies flat against the body. He runs with a characteristic horse-like double suspension gait which means all paws are off the ground at the same time. While running, the tail straightens out for greater balance. They are known as the barkless dog. They make a low howl/moaning/yodeling sound.

YOU MAY HAVE MANY BEST FRIENDS BUT YOUR DOG HAS ONLY ONE ❤

Temperament

The Basenji is known as the barkless dog. He does make other vocal sounds. He can howl, yodel, growl or crow depending on how he is feeling. Some of it can sound like human laughter or crying. This dog rarely pants. They clean themselves just like a cat. They spend hours grooming themselves and they have no doggie smell. They cope well with wet conditions but hate the rain and wet weather. The Basenji is very powerful for his size. They are also tireless, speedy and very attentive. They need a daily walk as they can become fat and lazy. This dog is intelligent and independent. This dog needs to be socialized when young. Start as soon as you can. Take your dog out and introduce him to new people, children, other pets and loud noises. Keep doing this as your dog grows and you will have a much calmer dog that is not shy at all. They do not like to be left alone, so if you cannot spend lots of time with him, he may need another pal or two to be with him but he does not do well with non canine animals. They prefer to live in a pack. They do love all children and are very warm and affectionate. They have a very gentle nature. They are wary of strangers but bonds well with his family. If they get bored they can become destructive, so make sure they have lots of chew toys to play with. They love to chew everything. They are also climbers and escape artists. They will definitely try to climb the fence. They always seem to find a way out of the yard.

The Basenji is considered to be a sight hound, so he has excellent eye sight and their sense of smell is also extraordinary. They were bred to be hunters and can chase down any thing with ease. The Basenji is fine living in an apartment as long as he gets enough exercise during the day. A long daily walk will do. They are very independent and can play alone sometimes.

Health

Not all Basenjis will have these health problems but it is important that you know about them. Find a responsible breeder. Your puppy's parents should have health clearances. These clearances prove that the parents have been tested for certain conditions. You can find the health clearances online at www.offa.org. This is the Orthopedic Foundation for Animals. They test for hip dysplasia, elbow dysplasia, and knees.

Progressive Retinal Atrophy (PRA) in Dogs

Progressive Retinal Atrophy (PRA) is an inherited disease of the retina in dogs, in which the eyes will go blind. PRA occurs in both eyes at the same time and is not painful. Both parents have to have it for their puppies to get it. It doesn't usually appear until the dog is between four and seven years old. Check with your veterinarian.

Hip Dysplasia

Hip Dysplasia is a genetic flaw in all dogs. It can happen to a dog at any age but usually happens in larger dogs that grow quickly. Find out about your puppies parents. Dog breeders should have a set of x-rays taken of the mother and the father taken at 2 years of age to see if their dogs have hip dysplasia. If they do have hip dysplasia they should not be bred. The results of these x-rays can be seen at www.offa.org The breeder should also be able to show certificates that the parents are okay. With Hip Dysplasia the hip joint fits poorly into the socket. As the dogs gets older the joint will become wobbly making the joint have tenderness and pain. All activity for the dog is painful. The dog will be less mobile and will have difficulty getting up. This condition can be treated medically or surgically. The veterinarian will decide depending on how severe it is. Basenjis should not be allowed to get over-weight.

Hypo-Thyroid

This is when the thyroid is acting sluggish and can cause weight gain, lethargy, poor hair coat, infertility and chronic infections. See your veterinarian.

Fanconi Syndrome

Fanconi Syndrome is unusually common in Basenji's. With this inheritable disorder, the kidneys fail to reabsorb electrolytes and nutrients. Symptoms include excessive drinking, excessive urination. There may be glucose in the urine which could lead to a misdiagnosis of diabetes. It can show up as early as three years of age to as late as ten years of age. This is treatable and organ damage is reduced if treatment is started early. See your veterinarian.

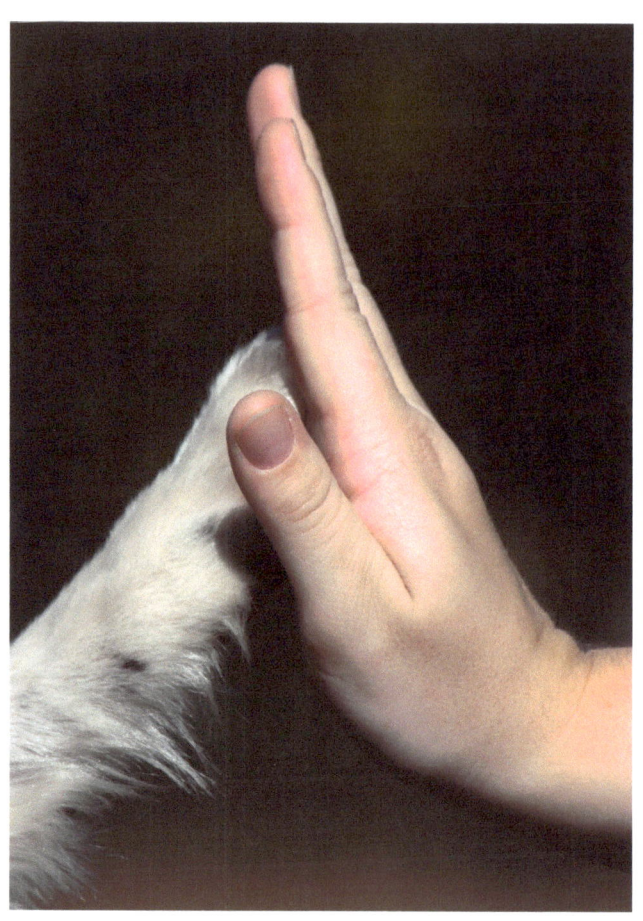

"Discover How You Can Insure That Your Dog Is The Healthiest Pet Alive!"

Dear Dog Owner,

If you were asked if your dog is healthy and happy, how would you respond? Do you really know how to "read" your pet?

"Fido" can't speak for himself and relies on you to be his eyes and ears for everything in his or her world. That means everything, from what is the best diet to reading the signs of illness.

Sounds like "easier said than done," doesn't it?

Well, we can't teach you how to speak "canine," but we can give you the tools to reach a better understanding of what life is like for your pet.

Starting today, learn the facts about what your dog really needs to survive longer and healthier.

If you are looking for a book on how to train your pet or how to engage in obedience training, this is not the book for you.

How to Have a Healthy Dog is for the dog owner who wants to better understand the health of their pet so they know when it is appropriate to take serious action to assist a vulnerable or ailing dog.

Did you know?

Dogs shouldn't be given chocolate? Do you know why?
Dogs get allergies just like people. Can you identify them?

How to give your dog CPR?

Are you giving your dog nutritional food? Walk down the aisle in the grocery stores and you will see every kind of dog food that you can imagine.

Are you randomly selecting your pets diet based on what's the cheapest? Go ahead, admit it. . .most of us do, but we are really short changing our pet when we buy based on cost.

Discover what the best food is for your pet, not the thousands of other dogs on the planet. By all means, comparison shop, but don't cut your pet short on his diet to save a few pennies.

How to Have a Healthy Dog will reveal what you need to do in order to assure that your pet is getting the proper nutrients for his size and age. Remember. .knowledge really is **power!**

Down to the "nitty gritty"

Do you think that you have taken every precaution to see to it that your dog does not become ill? Well, let's see. Are you under the impression that "distemper" and "rabies" are the same illness?

You'd be surprised how many people believe they are the same. They aren't and each needs to be treated properly. We've all been there and believe we know everything there is to know about our pets. Unfortunately, that isn't the case.

More Burning Questions. . .

Is it true that dogs can cough?

- What are intestinal parasites?
- Should we feed our dog meat, carbohydrates or fat?
- How can we control flea infestation?
- What is heartworm?
- What is Leptosporosis?

We are all familiar with the "standard" diseases that we hear about in dogs. But, rabies, distemper and parvo are not the only diseases our dogs are vulnerable to. There are others that, while they are familiar in the veterinary world, we know nothing about. See if you can identify these:

Canine kennel cough

Infectious Canine Hepatitus

Canine Coronavirus

Lyme disease

Get the answers to these questions and much more from **How to Have a Healthy Dog**. Don't wait. Grab the information you need to put your pet on the road to good health and nutrition!

Enjoy Your Dog and ensure he has a healthy life!

[Check out this book](http://www.divinedogsonline.com/product/how-to-have-a-healthy-dog/)

http://www.divinedogsonline.com/product/how-to-have-a-healthy-dog/

Care

The Basenji has a fine short coat. They clean themselves like a cat and they shed very little. Feed your dog top quality dog food so that he gets all the vitamins and minerals that he needs. Brush your dog's teeth twice a week to remove the accumulation of plaque and tartar that can cause cavities and periodontal disease. Clip their nails on a regular basis. Take your dog for a brisk walk every day and play mental exercises with him. The Basenji is an indoor dog and should not be left out in a kennel.

To my dog

I will never move and not take you with me
I will never put you in a shelter and leave
I will never let you starve
I will never let you hurt
I will never desert you when you get old
Nor will I leave you when you go blind
If that time comes I will be there to hold you
Because I love you and you are FAMILY

©The Brunson Chronicles

Breeders

Find yourself a reputable breeder. If you don't know of one, ask your veterinarian, go to a dog show or check the internet. If you find a good breeder on the internet they can send you pictures of their puppies and parents. When I got my big guy King, the breeder sent me pictures every week so that I could see his progress. It was so exciting; I could hardly wait for him to arrive. If you can find a breeder close to you, go and visit the kennels to see how clean they are and meet the parents. Never buy a dog from a pet store or a puppy mill. They will not know if the parents are healthy or if the puppy is healthy. A breeder will have the parents tested for any health issues that can be passed on to the puppy. When you contact your breeder ask to see these clearances. Some of the clearances can be found at http://www.offa.org . Ask your breeder lots of questions. Ask about anything that you would like to know. Things like history, health issues, food to feed. The breeder will not mind at all. They love to talk about their dogs. The breeder will also have questions for you. They want to know that their puppy is going to its forever home and that it will fit in with you, your family and your lifestyle. The breeder will also have a contract for you to sign. It will lay out what is your responsibility and what is the breeder's responsibility. Most breeders will include a health guarantee on the puppy for a certain length of time and usually the breeder will include a clause for first right to refusal. This means that if you can no longer keep your dog, the breeder wants the first right to get it back. Think carefully about getting your dog. You will be responsible for this little bundle of fur for 12 years. That is a long time. If you are unsure at all if you can do this, let some one else have this puppy. You can adopt an older dog from a rescue that would love to go home with you.

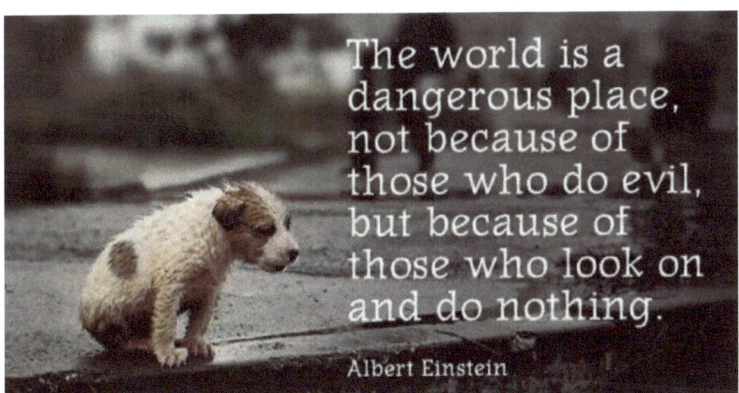

Training

Basenji's need firm and consistent leadership. Make sure that your dog knows that you are the alpha dog, not him. Positive reinforcement works the best for this dog. Teach your dog a command and then ask him to do it. If he does it praise him, give him a treat. When he realizes that he will get praise for doing what you ask, he will easily do it. They only want to please. If your dog doesn't do what you want, just ignore him and ask again. Never hit or yell at your dog. Dogs are sensitive and they will become afraid of you and be timid. This is hard to reverse. This dog can be quite mischievous and should be taught "no". Socialize your dog as soon as possible. Take him out and introduce him to new people, children, other pets and loud noises. Keep doing this as he grows and he will be a calmer, less timid dog. Obedience training is necessary for this dog. You can go to obedience training classes, hire a trainer or train your dog yourself. They are very intelligent so training should be quite easy. Be consistent with your training. Make your sessions fun and only for 15 to 20 minutes. Any longer and the dog will be thinking of something else. Make sure there are no distractions during training. Start with one word commands, such as sit, stay, down and come. Only train one command at a time and stay on it until the dog has it. If you try and train too many commands at once, the dog will become confused.

Start potty training as soon as you bring your puppy home. Pick out a spot where you would like the dog to go potty. Also pick out a phrase to say when the dog goes potty. Something like "Go Potty". When you see your dog start to go potty, pick him up, take him to the spot and say your phrase. If you watch your puppy, he will tell you when he has to go potty. He will start to sniff the floor, then walk around in circles before he

squats. When you see him start to do this take him out to his spot. Take him out as soon as he wakes up in the morning, right after he eats, right after he plays, right after he drinks. Anytime that you think he might have to go. You will probably have to get up at night for a while. Just like having a baby.
Puppies do not have full control of their bladder until about 4 months of age. Smaller dogs may take a bit longer. Never rub your dog's nose in his potty. He will not know why you are doing it

Some people like to use crate training for potty training. The idea is that a dog will never go potty where it sleeps. This is true unless they can no longer hold it. If you use a crate, do not leave your dog in there for to long. Only leave the puppy in the crate for an hour or two to start and work up from there. When you first get your crate, put in a nice soft blanket and a lot of chew toys to keep him busy. You can put the dog in the crate when you are going out so that he will not chew your belongings. Never put the dog in the crate as a punishment. You want the dog to like going into the crate. Almost like going into his own room, his own space.
A well trained dog is a joy to have.

Training Your Dog

With "Training Your Dog", you as a dog owner will be able to do more for your dog in terms of getting them to do what you need them to do. They need to learn to be obedient and do whatever you say, within reason. They need to understand that you are the dog owner and that they are to respect you as such. They need to get the message that disobedience will no longer be the norm in your household.

It's better to start training them when they are still a puppy. It's also easier to start when they are still young. The longer you wait, the more difficult it will be to get them to comply too your demands. Dogs are like children. You have to teach them what they need to do. When they do it wrong, you have to discipline and correct them to do it the right way.

You need to communicate to your dog what behavior is acceptable and what behavior is off limits. They need to know where you stand in everything. You have to be consistent and make sure that they know you mean business.

$9.98

Check this book out!

http://www.divinedogsonline.com/product/training-your-dog/

Origins

The Basenji can be traced back to ancient Egypt. They were brought up the Nile from Central Africa as gifts for the Pharaohs. They were painted within the tombs. The first recorded tomb drawing was within Khufu's Great Pyramid. It was erected in 2700 B.C. The breed disappeared and was found again in 1870 AD. The Basenji was discovered in Central Africa. The African tribes Mangbetu and Azande used these dogs to chase game into nets. Around 1930, these dogs were imported to the United States and England. The American Kennel Club accepted them as a breed in 1943. Basenji means "bush thing". The Basenji's were almost wiped out in the United States in the 1980's. The cause was Fanconi's Syndrome which is hereditary. Breeders went to the Congo to bring back more dogs that were free of this disease.

Some Registries

Basenji Club of America

http://www.basenji.org/

[Basenji Club of Great Britain](http://www.basenjiclubofgb.org/)

[The **Basenji Club** of New South Wales Inc.](http://www.basenjiclubnsw.org/)

[**Basenji Club** of Canada](http://www.basenjiclubofcanada.com/)

[Basenji Club Nederland Voorwoord](http://www.basenji-club.nl/)

[The Northern Basenji Society |](http://www.northernbasenji.org.uk/)

[Willamette Valley **Basenji Club**](#)

http://www.basenji-club.com/

Evergreen Basenji Club based in the Seattle/Tacoma area

http://www.evergreenbasenjiclub.org/

Mid-Atlantic Basenji Club

http://www.mabasenji.org/

Basenji Club of Cincinnati

http://www.angelfire.com/oh3/bcoc/

UKC United Kennel Club

http://www.ukcdogs.com/

NKC National Kennel Club

http://www.nationalkennelclub.com/

[CKC Continental Club](http://www.ckcusa.com/)

[CKC Canadian Kennel Club](http://www.ckc.ca/)

[APRI Americas Pet Registry Inc](http://www.aprpets.org/)

[AKC American Kennel Club](http://www.akc.org/)

[FCI Federation Cynologique Internationale](http://www.fci.be/)

NZKC New Zealand Kennel Club

http://www.nzkc.org.nz/

KCGB Kennel Club of Great Britain

http://www.thekennelclub.org.uk

ANKC Australian National Kennel Club

http://www.ankc.org.au

ACR American Canine Registry

http://www.americancanineregistry.com/

http://www.divinedogsonline.com

http://www.facebook.com/divine.dogs.online

http://www.pinterest.com/divinedogsonlin

http://www.adoreyourdogbyvideo.com

www.ingramcontent.com/pod-product-compliance
Lightning Source LLC
Chambersburg PA
CBHW042218050426
42453CB00001BA/8